HEALTHY CHOICES

Snacks

Vic Parker

raintree

a Capstone company — publishers for children

Raintree is an imprint of Capstone Global Library
Limited, a company incorporated in England and Wales
having its registered office at 7 Pilgrim Street, London,
EC4V 6LB – Registered company number: 6695582

www.raintreepublishers.co.uk
myorders@raintreepublishers.co.uk

Edited by Rebecca Rissman, Dan Nunn,
    and Diyan Leake
Designed by Philippa Jenkins
Original illustrations © Capstone Global
    Library Ltd 2014
Picture research by Tracy Cummins
Production by Helen McCreath
Originated by Capstone Global Library Ltd
Printed and bound in China

ISBN 978 1 406 27198 0 (hardback)
17 16 15 14 13
10 9 8 7 6 5 4 3 2 1

ISBN 978 1 406 27203 1 (paperback)
18 17 16 15 14
10 9 8 7 6 5 4 3 2 1

Parker, Vic
Snacks (Healthy Choices)
A full catalogue record for this book is available from
the British Library.

Acknowledgements
We would like to thank the following for permission to
reproduce photographs: Capstone Publishers (Karon
Dubke) pp. 4, 7, 8, 9, 10, 11, 12, 13, 14, 15, 16, 17,
18, 19, 20, 21, 22, 23, 24, 25, 26, 27; Shutterstock
pp. 5 (© Diego Cervo), 6 (© Shestakoff).

Cover photograph of chopped vegetables and sauce
on a plate reproduced with permission of Shutterstock
(© Africa Studio) and crisps reproduced with permission
of Shutterstock (© valzan).

Every effort has been made to contact copyright
holders of material reproduced in this book. Any
omissions will be rectified in subsequent printings if
notice is given to the publisher.

All the internet addresses (URLs) given in this book were
valid at the time of going to press. However, due to the
dynamic nature of the internet, some addresses may
have changed, or sites may have changed or ceased to
exist since publication. While the author and publisher
regret any inconvenience this may cause readers, no
responsibility for any such changes can be accepted by
either the author or the publisher.

Contents

 Some words are shown in bold, **like this.** You can find out what they mean by looking in the glossary.

Why make healthy choices?

Food is fuel for our bodies. We need food in order to think, move, and grow. To work properly, our bodies need different kinds of foods, in the right amounts for our age and size.

Your body also needs plenty of water every day.

Making healthy
choices helps you
keep well and happy.

Eating healthy foods helps you to
feel well and have lots of energy. It
helps you to think quickly and clearly.
It helps you look your best, too.

What makes a snack healthy or unhealthy?

Eating a snack is a good way to keep up your energy between meals. However, some snacks are much less healthy than others. For instance, salty snacks such as crisps are high in **sodium**, which is bad for your heart.

High-sugar snacks can give you **tooth decay**.

The amount of calories in a food is usually written on its packaging.

2 chocolate biscuits
around 300 calories

1 orange
around 100 calories

The energy food gives us is measured in **calories**. Each of us needs a certain amount of calories per day to stay healthy, depending on your age, your size, and how active you are. If you eat too many calories, you may become **overweight**. If you eat too few, you may become too thin.

Fruit

Fruit is very good for you. However, **processed** fruit snacks often contain unhealthy added ingredients. Extra sugar adds **calories** but does not make the snacks filling. **Artificial additives** such as **flavouring, colouring,** and **preservatives** are **chemicals** that have little goodness and can even be harmful.

added sugar

added artificial colouring, flavouring, and preservatives

Some processed fruit snacks are more like sweets than fruit.

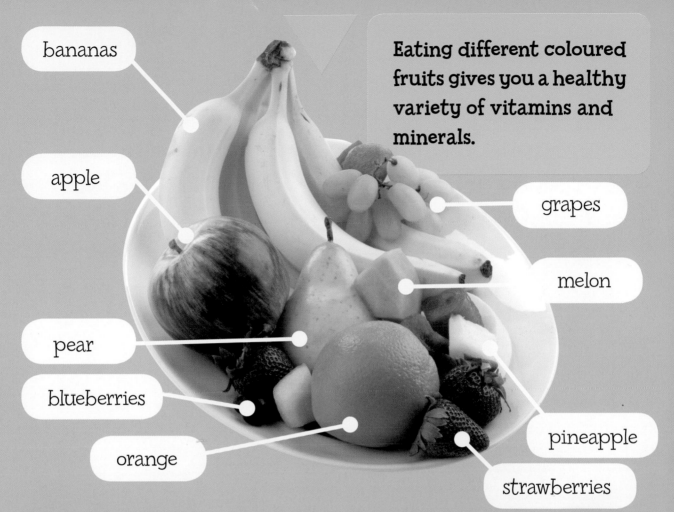

bananas

apple

grapes

melon

pear

blueberries

pineapple

orange

strawberries

Eating different coloured fruits gives you a healthy variety of vitamins and minerals.

Fresh fruit is a healthier choice. It contains natural sugar, which gives you energy. Fruit is packed with **vitamins, minerals,** and **antioxidants.** Your body can use these to grow, repair itself, and resist illness. Fruit also has plenty of **fibre,** which keeps your **digestive system** working properly.

Cheese

Cheese contains **calcium**, which builds strong bones and teeth. However, many cheeses, such as full-fat Cheddar, are high in **saturated fat**, which clogs the heart and blood vessels. Cheese can also be high in **sodium** and **calories**.

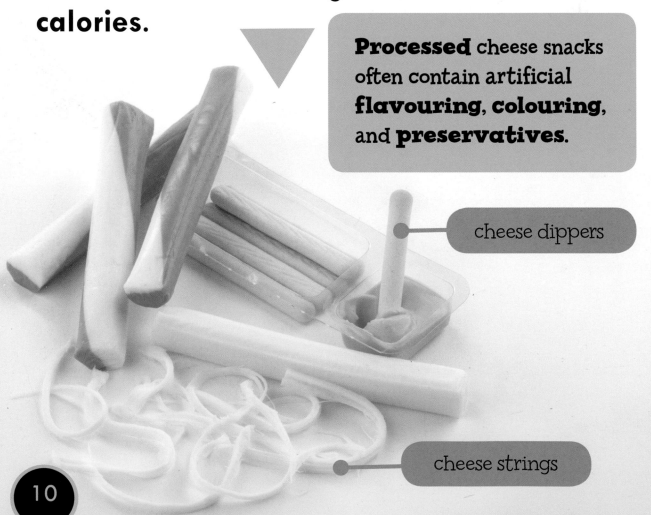

Processed cheese snacks often contain artificial **flavouring**, **colouring**, and **preservatives**.

cheese dippers

cheese strings

low-sodium
cottage cheese

grapes

Low-fat, low-calorie, low-sodium cheeses
are a healthy choice. These include feta,
mozzarella, Emmental, and low-fat Cheddar
cheese. Eat just a small portion, with some
fresh fruit for added energy, **vitamins**,
minerals, and **fibre**.

Biscuits

Everyone loves biscuits but they usually contain white flour, which is low in **fibre** and **vitamins**. Biscuits are also often high in **saturated fat** and sugar.

sugar

white flour

butter

Biscuits are tasty for an occasional treat, but not healthy as an everyday snack.

Homemade oatmeal biscuits can be a healthy alternative. Use a recipe with **wholemeal** flour, which is high in fibre and vitamins. Use vegetable oil instead of butter and use honey or dried fruit instead of sugar.

vegetable oil

wholemeal flour

oat flakes

honey

raisins

Homemade oat biscuits can be both delicious and healthy.

Popcorn

Popcorn is kernels of maize that are heated till they puff up and burst. Shop-bought popcorn that is coated thickly in sugary or **savoury flavourings** can be extremely high in **calories, saturated fat,** and **sodium.**

buttered popcorn

toffee popcorn

salted popcorn

sweet popcorn

There are many unhealthy kinds of popcorn.

chocolate popcorn

cheese popcorn

Balsamic vinegar and cinnamon are tasty, healthy toppings for homemade popcorn.

balsamic vinegar

cinnamon

Popcorn made at home can be very healthy. As a **wholegrain** food, it is high in **fibre**. Without coatings, it is low in saturated fat, calories, and sodium. It is also high in **antioxidants** — natural **chemicals** that strengthen your body's ability to fight disease.

15

Crisps

Potatoes can be good for you, but not when they are fried. Potato crisps are high in **saturated fat**, **sodium**, and **calories**. Baked, unsalted vegetable crisps are healthier, but still not as healthy as fresh vegetables.

Vegetables lose their goodness when they are made into crisps. Unhealthy ingredients are added to them, too.

beetroot crisps

parsnip crisps

sweet potato crisps

potato crisps

carrot crisps

Crunchy rice cakes are a healthier choice as they are low in fat and calories. Buy the unflavoured type and add your own healthy toppings.

Rice cakes are filling and they stop you feeling hungry between meals.

cinnamon

hummus

peanut butter

fruit purée

Yoghurt

Like cheese, yoghurt is a good source of **calcium**, for healthy bones and teeth. However, full-fat yoghurt is high in **saturated fat**. **Processed** yoghurts contain many **artificial additives** that are unhelpful or even harmful to your body.

added **flavouring**

high in fat

added **preservatives**

high in sugar

added **colouring**

There are many unhealthy types of yoghurt.

Low-fat natural yoghurt is healthy because much of the saturated fat has been taken out and no artificial additives put in. This sort of yoghurt can help your stomach to work properly and can even help your body fight **infection**.

wholegrain cereals

Add your own healthy flavourings to natural yoghurt.

raisins

nuts

fresh fruit

honey

Dips

Some people think that corn crisps are a healthy snack if they are eaten with an avocado or tomato dip. However, corn crisps are not much lower in **saturated fat** than potato crisps. They are also high in **sodium**.

soured cream

tomato dip

cheese

corn crisps

avocado dip

Corn crisps are especially unhealthy when they are smothered in high-fat cheese and soured cream, as nachos.

It is much healthier to eat vegetables, instead of corn crisps, with dips. Dips made at home from fresh ingredients are healthier than shop-bought ones which can contain **artificial additives** such as **colouring** and **preservatives**.

broccoli

hummus

tomato dip

avocado dip

carrots

cherry tomatoes

sugar-snap peas

Freshly homemade dips are tasty and healthy.

Sweet treats

Although many of us find chocolate delicious, it is usually made with added milk and sugar, which means that it is high in fat and **calories**. Also, milk and white chocolate contain little or no healthy **fibre**.

milk chocolate

white chocolate

Milk and white chocolate are not filling snacks.

If you crave a sweet treat, try a banana or dried fruit. These are packed with natural sugar. Eat just a few squares of dark chocolate made with more than 70 per cent **cocoa solids,** as this has less fat and sugar than milk or white chocolate, and contains a little fibre.

The healthiest chocolate choice is dark chocolate that contains fruit or nuts, for added **vitamins** and **minerals**.

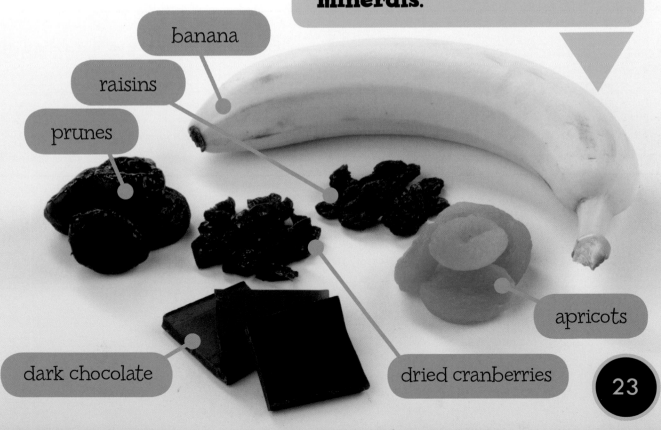

banana

raisins

prunes

apricots

dark chocolate

dried cranberries

Drinks

Milkshakes contain **calcium** for strong bones and teeth, and **protein** for healthy skin and muscles. Smoothies are packed with **vitamins** and **minerals**. However, milkshakes are also high in fat, and smoothies can be high in sugar. This makes them both high-**calorie** drinks.

milk, ice cream, whippedcream,sugary sprinkles

fruit **concentrate**, added syrup, sugar, sweetened yogurt

Milkshakes and smoothies can contain more calories than some desserts.

Water is the best drink at snack time. You can mistake thirst for hunger, so if you drink water you may not need a snack at all. Also, your body loses water all the time, so you need to replace it to stay well.

Flavour water with slices of fresh fruit.

ice

orange

lemon

lime

water

Food quiz

Take a look at these snacks. Can you work out which picture shows unhealthy snacks and which shows healthy snacks, and why?

water

raw mixed nuts

fresh blueberries

The answer is on the next page.

fizzy drink

blueberry muffin

pretzels

Food quiz answers

These are the healthy snacks. The mixed raw nuts and blueberries are packed with **fibre, vitamins,** and **minerals.** They are also high in energy, but low in **sodium.** Every bit of your body needs water to work properly.

These are the unhealthy snacks. The pretzels will give you energy but they are high in sodium. The blueberry muffin is high in **saturated fat** and sugar and low in fibre and vitamins. The fizzy drink is high in sugar and in **artificial additives** such as **colouring** and **flavouring.** Did you guess correctly?

Tips for healthy eating

Use this eatwell plate guide to choose the right amounts of different foods for good health. Choose low-fat cooking methods and do not add salt (it is high in **sodium**). Don't forget to drink several glasses of water and to exercise every day.

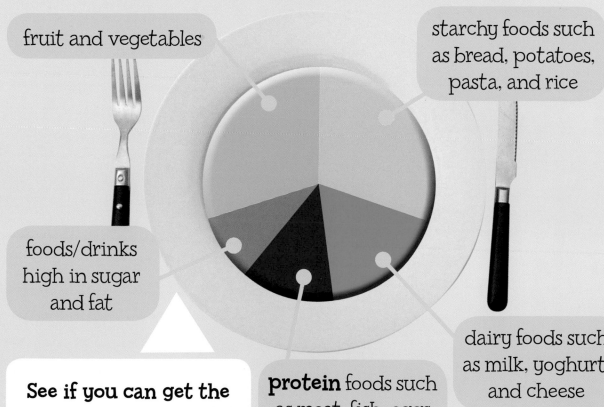

fruit and vegetables

starchy foods such as bread, potatoes, pasta, and rice

foods/drinks high in sugar and fat

dairy foods such as milk, yoghurt, and cheese

See if you can get the right balance over the course of a whole day.

protein foods such as meat, fish, eggs and beans

Glossary

antioxidant substance that helps your body fight off disease

artificial additive man-made substance that is added to food, such as colouring, flavouring, and preservatives

calcium a mineral our bodies need to build strong bones and teeth. Calcium is found in dairy foods and some vegetables, nuts, and seeds.

calorie unit we use for measuring energy

chemical substance made by mixing other substances together

cocoa solids chocolate that has had the cocoa butter taken out

colouring something added to food to make it look attractive

concentrate juice that has had most of the water taken out so that it lasts longer

digestive system all the body parts that break down food so the body can use it

fibre part of certain plants that passes through your body without being broken down. This helps other foods to pass through your stomach, too.

flavouring something added to food to make it taste nicer

infection disease caused by germs

mineral natural substance, such as iron, that is essential for health

overweight heavier than is healthy for your age and size

preservative something added to food to make it last longer

processed made or prepared in a factory. Processed foods often contain artificial additives.

protein a natural substance that our bodies need to build skin, muscle, and other tissues. Protein is found in foods such as meat, fish, and beans.

saturated fat type of fat found in butter, fatty cuts of meat, cheese, and cream. It is bad for your heart and blood.

savoury having a salty or spicy, rather than sweet, taste

sodium a natural substance found in salt

tooth decay bad teeth, caused by the outer layers of the teeth being dissolved away

vitamin natural substance that is essential for good health

wholegrain made with every part of the grain, without removing any of the inner or outer bits

wholemeal food made from ground-down whole grains

Find out more

Books

All About Fruit (Food Zone), Vic Parker (QED, 2010)
Be Good to Your Body: Healthy Eating and Fun Recipes,
  Roz Fulcher (Dover Publications, 2012)
Grow Your Own Snack (Grow It Yourself!), John Malam
  (Raintree, 2011)

Websites

Try some healthy recipes at: **www.bbcgoodfood.com/
content/recipes/healthy/healthy-kids**

Try some healthy eating activities at: **www.familylearning.
org.uk/balanced_diet.html** and **www.bbc.co.uk/
northernireland/schools/4_11/uptoyou/index.shtml**

Find out more about the eatwell plate healthy eating
guidelines at: **www.nhs.uk/Livewell/Goodfood/Pages/
eatwell-plate.aspx**

Index